Meet Me On the Other Side

Miracles from the Afterlife

Meet Me On the Other Side

Miracles from the Afterlife

STEFFANY BARTON, RN

gatekeeper press

Columbus, Ohio

Meet Me On the Other Side: Miracles from the Afterlife

Published by Gatekeeper Press
2167 Stringtown Rd, Suite 109
Columbus, OH 43123
www.GatekeeperPress.com

ISBN: 9781642370102

Printed in the United States of America

Contents

Author's Note

A MIRACLE.
    Chances are you've heard about one, prayed for one, witnessed one, or, if you're lucky, experienced one.

But what is a miracle, really?

Something magical, something grand, a wild and unprecedented event that leaves the experts befuddled and the non-believers awestruck?

Something inconceivable, something mystical, something completely random and unpredictable, a situational, circumstantial, supernatural wish come true?

Something for the religious, or pious, or those who have paid penance, something somehow secretly earned on the sly?

What is a miracle?

And can we learn to create them, to claim the power to accept them, to find the courage to believe that miracles are not earned, simply received?

Let's face it: Sometimes it's easy in life to lose sight, to go blind, to fall asleep behind the wheel. We whiz around, anticipating others' demands, striving to fit everyone's expectations, accommodating, acquiescing, working, sacrificing, resigning, sometimes dying to find significance, meaning in our lives.

Security is defined by money, a good job, a decent partner, smiling kids, a nice house, a manicured yard, Facebook friends, Twitter followers, YouTube subscribers. Click if you like . . . ..

Dressmaker's dummies posed in the world's façade, we play the part, living at arms' length. We tune in to the outside, investing in transient, tempestuous stock.

Then, when the job ends, when the money runs out, when the partner leaves and kids move out, when the yard overgrows, and social media implodes, what then? Is it over?

No! In fact, when the world seems to fall apart, often our soul has cleared the way for miracles.

Many years ago, a package arrived in my mailbox. Pulling it from the receptacle, I noted how depilated, torn, and damaged this parcel was. With a mangled corner, loose wrapping on the bottom, a return address that was obscured, I barely discerned the box was addressed to me.

Because I couldn't ascertain the origin of the package, and since I could not readily recall ordering anything soon to arrive, I took the box in and left it on a high shelf above the kitchen counter. I quickly forgot the bruised package; out of sight out of mind.

Months later, while cleaning, I rediscovered the unsightly box. Now curious, I opened it with caution. Inside, much to my delight and surprise, lay a golden, heart-shaped box. I had ordered it months and months prior, and had lost track of the purchase. The abused package offered a treasure, an open heart inside.

Sometimes in life, we feel like the box, all tattered and worn, forgotten, mistreated and mishandled. Disease demolishes the body, anxiety and stress causes us to come undone. Though the box, like the body, is the obvious packaging, the most noticeable feature, there is more, so much more to us than meets the eye.

Where does the oyster keep the pearl? Where in the chest

is the treasure? The cream of the donut? The butterfly and the cocoon?

On the *inside*. Just like the heart shaped box, contained within the mangled parcel, the truth of you, the essence of you, the *miracle* of you is always gently nestled inside, in an immutable heart of gold. Forget it, neglect it, bump, break or bruise it, it's there. You, the best of you, remains, unchanged, deep within the heart.

So what is a miracle?

I believe miracles are not so much about what transpires on the surface, nor defined by the exterior presentation. A miracle happens every time we reclaim that goodness, that purity, that utterly sweet and sublimely deep peace that is eternally, patiently, always waiting *inside*.

The story I share with you in this book is true. I have, out of respect for the privacy of the family and children, changed the first names. I never met either of the two central characters face-to-face; that was not the point. The days and nights I shared with them happened beyond time, in the eternal space of the heart.

I received a gift, a blessing in disguise. I learned, laughed, and cried with a stranger. I discovered that love is so much more than I had imagined, and that we are endlessly capable of giving goodness, kindness, and compassion into the world. I learned to trust more, to talk less, and to listen to the language beyond words. I came to understand that disease, sickness, and illness are not value indicators. I witnessed, first hand, a miracle.

I share my journey with you because I learned so much. I pray my story will give you a greater understanding of death, and soften the harshness of physical loss. More, though, I pray, heart and soul, this book will teach you about life, and how to live, fully, from the heart.

A miracle.

CHAPTER 1

Goodbye

HOW COULD IT end this way?

How could a man, larger than life, filled to overflowing with a sheer zest for living, get snagged in a web of suffering and pain.

How could he, of all men, die?

Jack strode around, a ruggedly rough and handsome cowboy, guided by principles, ever true to his word. He loved God and country, fiercely protected his family. Ceaselessly, he shared his good fortune with the community and showered lavish gifts on those he loved. He was a man among men.

And his laugh! The uproarious peals of his laughter would fill the room. Sparkling eyes, dazzling smile, tall and strong, he was built to last.

His wife, huddled at the bedside, fought back fiery hot tears. Flashes of first dates, trail rides, vacations, celebrations, and anniversaries haunted and comforted her all at the same time. With vows they proclaimed, "Til death do us part," but the truth: Neither half of the glorious whole was supposed to die. Immunity, immortality. Love should stay alive.

His comfort now came is small measures: a small sip of water, a cool cloth to the brow, a gentle touch to the hand, a soft kiss to the cheek. No words exchanged, no strength to speak, he laid still. Time dragged on.

His son, grown and on his own, would arrive soon. Living states away, working full time, married with young children in the home, he kept up with his father's journey, yet remained faithful to his commitments. Sometimes, work is a nice escape from reality. Sometimes, the miles buffer the intensity, mute the inability to control. Sitting by and watching one we love languish and suffer torments the heart and depletes the soul. Best to stay busy, distracted at home.

In the weeks prior, he and his wife spoke of the next steps. She would stay and maintain what he worked so hard for. She would live as he wished, because she could not allow his dreams to die with him. That would be too much.

But what a waste! Why would someone so good, so strong, so devoted and true have to suffer, to be cut short? What sin could he have committed, what wrong was being righted in this sentence of illness? Why?

Questions were plentiful, but good answers were in short supply.

Why?

Before he had grown so weak, he promised her that, if he died, he would find a way to communicate with her, and with his son, too. Perhaps a spiritualist, or a medium could help him raise his spirit's voice in the physical world. Far-fetched? Maybe. But worth a shot.

The darkness was coming. His wife knew he was slipping.

"It's okay. I'll tell your son. Let go. I will be strong," she wept.

He stepped through the darkness, took a breath of life. In the light, he was home.

How could it end this way?

Only 44 years old, the sweetest, most loving woman, she was filled to overflowing with faith, hope, and life. Her strength lay in her quiet reserve; she inspired with grace and nurtured with kindness. She loved everyone.

I was blessed to call her my mom.

We lived in a small town in Missouri. She stayed at home, cooked, kept house, never asked for anything much, just love. And popcorn on Friday nights; that was her favorite treat.

She attended church regularly, and her devotion to Jesus was genuine, real. She prayed, laughed, and cried with the ladies in her Bible study group. I never heard her curse, never saw her yell in anger or strike out in haste. She was too gentle.

One summer, we found a walking stick bug on the screen door leading to the back patio. My younger sister and I both squealed—this bug was big! She took a shoe to shoo it, in so doing she unwittingly squashed it. She cried, apologized to the bug, and laid its body to rest in the backyard.

When my first pet goldfish died, she helped me find a suitable coffin. She stood with me as I spoke a few words of goodbye to Mendel Fish. She planted flowers at the tiny grave that summer.

She had a heart of gold and lungs tumor-filled. We didn't know until it was too late . . .

Three years prior to her death, she developed an odd, hacking cough. Our small-town doctor told her it was allergies and sent her home.

The cough persisted.

She did her best to adjust to it, as she was not one to complain. But after a year of chronic coughing, she returned to the doctor. She was tired; the cough often kept her up at night.

Again, the doctor dismissed her—she looked fine. Her

fatigue was easily explained by the lack of sleep. He sent her home with a cough suppressant, which she immediately tried.

It didn't work.

One day, she picked me up from school. She was unusually quiet; I asked her why.

"Something's wrong, Steffy. I don't know what it is, but I fear something's just not right," she spoke softly, keeping her eyes on the road.

"Mom, you're fine. I know you are. Come on, I'll treat you to Sonic," I offered. I was nearing high school graduation and worked a few hours a week at Kentucky Fried Chicken. I enjoyed having a bit of spending money.

"Thanks, honey. But I'm okay. You got a letter from the college today," she changed the subject, not a moment too soon. We were both relieved by the diversion.

I would attend classes at the local University that fall. My intention was to attain a degree in nursing. I loved people and wanted to help in any way I could. My mom was especially proud; I was the first person in the family to go to college.

As planned, my classes commenced in the autumn. I threw myself whole-heartedly into school and thrived in the progressive environment. I understood all the parts of anatomy, fully functioned in physiology, devoured the information in nutrition classes, and statistically speaking, did well in math. But the unexpected new love in my life was microbiology. Oh, I loved the little single cell guys!

With a year of college under my belt, and a perfect GPA, I felt invincible.

That's when the storm came.

One fateful afternoon, my mom decided to drive into town to see a new doctor. She didn't want to offend her regular provider, but the cough lingered and, in fact, had worsened. The turning point came when she coughed up a significant amount of blood and what appeared to be tissue.

The new doc ordered a chest x-ray and my mom shuffled to the radiology department. The test was quick, but the tech told her to wait a moment. She was instructed to go back to the office immediately. She followed orders.

The x-ray revealed a tumor roughly the size of a grapefruit on her left lung. Within a few hours, a pulmonologist was on the case. Consults were arranged, a surgeon brought on. This was serious business. Time was of the essence.

Two weeks later she was scheduled for left pneumonectomy. We were all shocked. This was not supposed to happen. Not to her. Not to anyone.

The surgeon advised us that the road to recovery would be a difficult one, and her time in recovery and ICU would be "hellish." Though she would have lots of pain medication, she would not be entirely comfortable, he stated. I appreciated his honesty; he made no attempt to sugarcoat the situation.

I attended classes the morning of her surgery because I couldn't bare the anxiety of sitting in the hospital, powerless, watching the clock. I wanted to have a "normal" day. After class, I scooted to the hospital to see her in the ICU. She wasn't there. She was in a regular room. My heart sank. This was wrong.

The only time I ever remember seeing her with a frown was that day. I softly entered her private room; she was groggy from the anesthesia. The corners of her mouth were downturned; her words from the year before came back to me, "Something is wrong. . . ."

I sat next to her and took her hand. She fluttered her eyes and a moment later, a nurse walked into the room.

"What happened? Why is she here? Why not ICU?" I asked.

"There was a complication, and I'll let the doctor go over everything with you," she replied.

In the operating room, with her chest open, the doctors discovered not only a grapefruit sized tumor, but cancer cells growing everywhere. In the operating suite, phone calls were made to an outside facility in Texas. All parties agreed that removing the lung was pointless. It was too far gone.

The next eight months were bleak. The horrible chemotherapy ravaged her body and did not even touch the cancer. Radiation only burned her skin; the cancer raged on.

To offer relief, the doctor would insert a chest tube every few weeks to drain fluid from her lung. I joined her at one of these appointments. The nurse lifted my mom's comfy, pink t-shirt and we all stood aghast. The tumor was protruding from her chest, burrowed through her skin and out the site of insertion. I turned my head, hoping to unsee the horrific sight. I wanted to take this from my mom.

That night, I pulled every microbiology book I could find from my shelf. I wanted to know how non-small cell squamous carcinoma in situ formed so I could craft a way to destroy it. Maybe the doctors couldn't do it, but perhaps I could. Far-fetched? Maybe, but worth a shot.

I couldn't sleep. I couldn't eat. All I could do was read and think and read and think about cancer of the lung. And how to kill it. I had to. I just had to before cancer killed my mom.

Yet, the more I thought about it, the less I understood. Endless questions fell into the answerless abyss. No inspiration, no insight, no cure would come.

Why would someone so good, so strong, so devoted and true have to suffer, to be cut short? What sin could she have committed, what wrong was being righted by this illness?

She did everything right. Prayer, good clean eating, lots of fresh air, meditation, plenty of good clean water. Preachers came to exorcise the cancer demon, but it callously persisted.

Why?

My sincere questions were plentiful, but good answers were in short supply.

Why?

On a hot summer day in June, I went to her. She was in the ER, intubated, bloated, unrecognizable, really. A shell was all that seemed to remain. A shell with cancer.

We knew this was the beginning of the end.

From the ER, she went to ICU. We were given the best option: Remove life support, let the nurses keep her comfortable. See her, say goodbye.

I would not, I could not, say goodbye.

The next morning, June 19th, Juneteenth, the same day slavery was abolished in 1865, she unlocked the dark chains of enslavement bound by cancer, took a breath of sweet freedom and sipped pure light. Free at last, she was home. She was home.

I didn't say goodbye.

My mom's death, or more rightly, her rebirth, was a rebirth for me too. In the months following her transition, I plunged helplessly, frighteningly into womb-like, tomb-like darkness. In pitch black, there's really no difference between conception and destruction, after all.

Just when I thought I, too, would slip away, when I entertained the allure of escape, when I yearned secretly and desperately to join her, forgotten memories flooded my heart and buried images resurfaced in my mind. My miracle, my freedom, sweet liberation had come.

When I was a child, I could see and talk to spirits. I didn't know how not to do this; I just did. I loved chatting with the nice people who came around. Some were quiet, some made absolutely no sound but would simply look at me.

When I would notice them and smile, they would seem to vanish, poof! Spirited away.

One day, with much enthusiasm, I shared some of these experiences with a friend at school. She told my teacher who told the principle who told my parents who told the minister. Before I could say "Good heavens!" I learned demons were following me and Satan was lurking about, preying on my soul. The news unsettled me, rattled me to the core. I swore never to speak again to a spirit.

I kept my word. Until I spoke with the spirit of my mom.

So unrelenting was the pain in losing her, and so delicious was the cure in finding her spirit that I decided to devote myself to sharing my ability with the world. After years of patience, prayers, meditation, and learning, I am at peace with the work I do. I contribute to the world by communicating messages from loved ones on the Other Side. In so doing, I can offer comfort, share hope, and shine light into the darkness of fear shrouding death. I am completely devoted to Spirit and dedicated fully to Love.

A son who lost a father. A daughter who lost her mom.

Death was a beginning for both.

CHAPTER 2

Introductions

TUGGING THE STICKY, stubborn peanut butter across the mangled slice of whole wheat bread, I felt the draft. With every hair on my neck standing on end, I knew I had company.

"I'm off duty, you know. My tummy is rumbling because it's lunch time. Can you come back in a bit, please? I have rules; you've been advised."

For a moment, silence. With impatience, I held my breath, then put a bready lid on the sad sandwich. The spirit had not budged. Speaking aloud, I asked, "Can I help you?"

"*Yes!*" came the immediate and urgent reply. "*Please, I truly need your help. Please, this is important. I wouldn't be here otherwise. But you're the one. You can help him.*"

"Who?" I whispered inquisitively while placing bread and peanut butter back in the cupboard.

"*My son. He's sick and very frightened. Please, will you help me help him.*"

A silence slipped between us. How could I say no?

In that moment, when a messenger from the heavens above spoke to the medium on the earth below, two worlds collided:

mine and his. Neither of us would be the same again as we forged ahead into a brave new world.

Not fully committed, nor willing yet to be, I nevertheless felt compelled, intrigued. A maternal tug, an empathic nudge, the spirit of compassion invoked from within me felt a strong sense of conviction. "Fearless," I whispered to myself. "I want to be fearless."

There are moments when, like an old, dusty, stiffened book, we must open our heart wide. Painful yet exhilarating, to fully live is to fearlessly love.

Directing my focus toward him, speaking from my shaking, pounding heart, I tentatively accepted, "I will see what I can do. I will see if I can help your son. I don't want to let him, or anyone down. I have a full schedule with sessions today. Can you come back later? Please?"

He was gone.

After lunch, my first client arrived. She was a bereaved daughter, the primary caretaker of her mother who had recently died. The daughter struggled with survival guilt, and wanted to know she had done enough.

Compounding her guilt was the heartbreak she endured as she watched her mother linger for two years with Alzheimer's disease. Her proud, witty, well-educated mother withered to a seemingly empty shell before she set her body aside. Rendered blind, she existed sightless in the months leading up to her transition.

The mother's spirit gladly, graciously stepped forward as there was much catching up to do. Her first message to her daughter proved healing for her heart and touching to her soul.

"Please tell my daughter I am very proud of her painting. I think she is a wonderful artist. And let her know I saw the roses, and the lilies. I loved all the clouds as well."

Her daughter looked at me incredulously, then explained,

"When I first entered college, years and years ago, I wanted to be an artist. My mom, well-meaning and looking out for me, discouraged that, strongly spoke against that. So, I became an accountant. Oh, it was hard. But I was successful and made good with my career. When my mom got sick, after she was unable to drive or leave the house, she was very confused. I would sit with her, making sure she was safe. Then I decided, with so much time there, I would try my hand at painting.

"It has been decades since I'd picked up a brush. Oh, but the joy and the color and the freedom in doing what I loved. Mom never protested or fought against it. She was too out of it to really know what I was doing. I did notice, however, then as I started painting, she would smile and relax. I thought it was a coincidence.

"As I finished a painting, I would hold it up and show her. I know she couldn't see . . . or at least I didn't think so. My first completed painting was Mom's roses. And right now, I'm working on the clouds. Are you saying she sees my paintings?" she asked through tears.

"*I see a great and beautiful thing, and I don't mean on the canvas. Yes, her work is wonderful, but my daughter is my miracle. I am so proud of my painter. Thank you!*" her mother's spirit declared.

"I am so happy for her. But please tell her I'm sorry she had to suffer so much. I tried to help her. I really did. But she didn't want to eat, she didn't dress herself. I prayed every day she wasn't hurting. Was she okay? What was happening during that time? Why did she have to go through that?" her daughter asked.

Her mother's spirit explained, "*My time spent in that state was vital for my growth. I was not suffering, I was considering, learning, accepting. During that time, I had to tune my awareness to the inside . . . that was a mysterious unknown! I had spent my life doing for others. The last few years were about me settling in and discovering my own soul,"* her mother explained. *"There was no pain or sadness because of the condition of my body. I had feelings, to be sure. But the experience of Alzheimer's taught me to forgive, to love, to make peace, then, to let go."*

"What my daughter gave me, her time and her love, was truly wonderful. But now, the best thing she could give me is a promise: I want her to paint with all her heart and soul!" her mother said.

The message of forgiveness, love, acceptance, and celebration brought a tremendous feeling of peace to the room. Her daughter agreed, "I promise mom, I'll never stop painting. You have my word," she concluded.

We spoke for a bit more, then her daughter asked a final question, "Who was there to meet her, to greet her on the Other Side?"

"Well, it was not your father, that's for sure! I had enough of him for all of eternity in this lifetime! I saw my Mother, and my son, your brother. That was very healing for me. It's good to feel whole inside," her mother explained.

Her daughter laughed heartily, "Oh my goodness! I am glad she didn't have to deal with my dad. You don't have to be married in heaven, do you? I mean, there are no weddings or births there, are there?" She asked.

"No," I shared what I had learned through talking with spirits daily, "We don't need weddings or vows or those Earthly arrangements. We're with the ones we love and everything flows beautifully. Even people we didn't agree with are cast in a much more favorable light. So, peace prevails on the Other Side,"

"I am glad!" she exclaimed. "Oh mom, I love you!"

We closed our time together.

After taking a quick break, I noticed my next client coming up the walk. She seemed a bit

nervous. I ushered her in and showed her my office space. "Welcome to the angel room," I said.

My office space reflects my inner whimsy and fairy-like playfulness. Vines drape from the ceiling, a wishing pond constructed of blue glass and fish aquarium gravel decorates the floor. Along the north wall, I entwined blue and white cloths, then tacked them along the wall. The effect gives the appearance of a cascade flowing into hollow landscape boulders, my own Angel Falls.

I cherish my space; it's a place of healing and comfort where each and all are warmly welcome and truly loved.

She sat across from me and expressed her anxiety. "I've never done this before," she confessed.

"Thank you for allowing me to serve you. I want you to ask questions, if you need to, as we go," I instructed her.

I couldn't hold back the spirits who wanted to connect with her. It was time for them to make their presence known.

The first spirit who stepped forward was a young boy, perhaps two years old. He used the word *mom,* so I gathered this was the spirit of her son. I asked, "Have you lost a little boy?"

She looked at me and confirmed, without making eye contact, "Yes, my son."

I relayed details from him that only she could know: favorite foods, silly songs, his lovey. She knew his spirit had joined us. Then, she asked an important question.

"I know he's with me. I truly accept that. But there is something that has weighed heavy on me since the time he died. He was so young. All his grandparents are here; he's really the first in our immediate family to die. Is he alone? Who welcomed him? Who takes care of him on the Other Side?" she asked.

Her son spoke, *"My puppy, of course!"* and he showed me a little golden dog. *"And angels. Mommy, I've never felt alone."*

His mother cried. A few weeks before her son passed, they had put the family dog to rest. The loyal and true companion had been poisoned, and would not survive the effects. She had never considered the two would pal around. "That makes me so happy! And it makes perfect sense," she stated.

"*No one is lonely here. I see myself in everyone I meet. We really are all a family! I am happy and free. I love you, Mommy,*" he spoke.

His mother affirmed her love for him. We spoke about him a bit further, and covered a few other topics of concern. The time together affirmed the power of Love and the gift of spirit. We are all family.

My next reading was over the phone, followed by a healing session. At the close of the work day, I felt tired, but satisfied. Dinner, then family time, then shower, then meditation time.

Then the night shift began.

Relaxing on the couch, I let my mind wander. I remembered the words from the little angel with whom I'd spoken about Love and family. At that moment, my visitor returned and our first lesson began.

"*Howdy, ma'am, pleased to see you again,*" he greeted me rather grandly, with an exaggerated drawl. "*Sorry about butting in earlier. I guess my enthusiasm got the best of me.*"

"Well, I forgive you. Happens all the time. You spirits keep odd hours, you know!" I smiled.

"*We met the other day, remember? I hope you do, because I've wanted to connect with you for a while,*" he said.

I searched my mind and came up blank. "I'm sorry, I don't remember you. I talk to a lot of people, though, physical and non. Who are you, please?"

"*What!! How could you forget me and my smile?*" he feigned offence at my shoddy memory. "*Think about it,*" he instructed.

Again, I could not recall his spirit, not readily at least.

"Okay, I give. Who are you?" I asked.

"*Your friend, your best friend. The other day in her session she asked about the spirit in her basement and the health of her cousin,"* he said.

Pulsing clouds of light, like thunderclouds in an electric storm, flickered in my mind: I saw flashes of a basement, pictures of horses, a coursing stream. I could hear birds and feel cool, crisp air breezing past me. Ah, the mountains. I remembered.

"You're JACK!" I stated. "I know you. Why are you here? Oh, my gosh, it IS you." I remembered him.

"In the flesh," he laughed. *"You know what I mean. It's good to see you!"*

"Uh, you too," I responded. "How can I help you?"

"My son is her cousin, the one she asked about. He is sick, very sick. He needs me, he needs you, he needs US. Will you help me?"

"He's done all the traditional techniques. He's been to a foreign country. He's tired . . . ."

I interrupted, "Wait a minute here! So, you're telling me I'm the last stop? When nothing else works . . . talk to the crazy lady? The last resort?"

"No. I would have been here sooner, but these things take time. Synchronicities, coincidences, crossing paths. Spirit works serendipitously. It takes time," he replied.

"So, he's scared. And uncertain. I can guide him. You can help him. He needs a miracle. We can give him one," the spirit replied.

I thought of how I could offer support in a way that would benefit the son.

I agreed to the job.

"Good! He needs us. He needs a miracle!"

I smiled, nodded my head and replied, "Miracles are my favorite. Consider it done!"

CHAPTER 3

Acceptance

"You're leaving your nursing job to do WHAT?" my friend asked incredulously. "Are you kidding? That is a step backwards. Didn't you start the nurse practitioner program?"

I heaved a sign and felt a knot in my stomach, my throat, my shoulders. In fact, as she finished her question, my whole body felt like one big knot.

"Well, I've taken some classes, and it seems to come pretty easy. I don't know. Maybe I'm crazy. But at least I need to try. I have to see," I explained, guarded.

I enjoyed nursing, and chose that as my profession for one reason: I love people and wanted to be a healing force for others. I had a good head on my shoulders, enjoyed adventure, possessed a strong constitution and needed little sleep. All things considered, nursing seemed a perfect fit for me.

For a while, I made due and enjoyed the work. But with the ever-quickening pace of health-care, with technology eclipsing more traditional modalities, I soon found myself drowning in charting, troubleshooting machinery, and running endlessly. A turning point came when, at the end of a shift, I realized that

I couldn't remember the names of any of my patients. I knew it was time for me to make a change.

Having a strong connection with my mom's spirit helped, as well as the experience with my class partner's spirit guide who communicated with me so freely. I decided to delve a little deeper, but I was a bit scared. I didn't exactly know what I was in for.

First, I found a local new age bookstore. As I walked toward the entrance of the little shop, I felt a mix of guilt, excitement, fear, and enthusiasm. I prayed I would be okay; I still had some of the old fears that something "evil" lurked about, waiting to snatch me.

The bookstore smelled earthy, musty, good. Crystal balls lined the front window, playfully catching sunbeams. A rainbow of tie dye apparel hung cheerily in the back. Amazing crystals and gemstones adorned an area near the front register. Oh, it felt like a long forgotten but sorely missed home.

I spent the entire afternoon there, drinking up all the information like a parched child on a hot summer day. I basked in the books like a lizard on a rock; I felt warmed, understood. Leaving the shop, I noticed a flyer, "Angel Class." The class took place the next day.

Arriving to the class a few minutes early, I chose a seat near the front. The next two hours were filled with information and discovery. Angels sprang to life, nevermore just a Christmas décor.

More courses, a few classes, then it was time. I took an ad out in the local new age newspaper. "Steffany Barton, RN. Angel readings."

I had a call, then another, then a few more. Clients referred friends, those friends became clients who referred their friends. Soon I was busy. My nursing days were over, and I never looked back.

A big break came when I had a session with a woman enrolled in the nurse practitioner program that I had briefly attended. Before I discovered angels, and my mediumship abilities, I considered an advanced nursing role. But, no matter how I tried, something always worked against me. When that door closed, the angels opened another—the door to my heart.

I sat with this woman, a professional peer, and shared with her messages from her father's spirit. I could see her aura, the energy field around her, which I described to her in detail. When we concluded our time together she asked, "Would you be a guest speaker for my class, please? I want my classmates to have a chance to hear about you and your abilities. Please?"

I diligently prepared a talk on the chakras for the nursing students. I related how our physical organ systems correspond and communicate with our energy "organ" system.

Within a few months of beginning my spiritual business, I built a bridge to my former profession in the "real" world. I felt good.

Still, the response of my friend, the "You left your job to do WHAT" pervaded, especially from family. I struggled with this quite a lot.

For some, speaking with the deceased is taboo, weird, or evil. That's fine. For others, there's no need to dwell on an afterlife when we're dealing with here and now, and that's fine, too. I am comfortable with my beliefs. My prayer is that all find the deep, peaceful, liberating comfort with personal beliefs, too.

When I learned to accept myself, I no longer felt compelled to meet the expectations of others. And, I felt relieved of the need to convince anyone of my authenticity. I know I am guided; I surrender, trust Spirit, and am directed. Self-acceptance is truly the key that unchains us from fear and sets our spirit free.

I had come to the place of accepting Jack's request, of speaking for his spirit, of sharing his desire to be a force of inspiration and hope for his son Brock, yet the true question remained:

Would Brock accept me? Could his son be open to my work? Would he willingly receive? Could he learn to believe? Would he accept me?

"*There's only one way to find out, Sunshine*," Jack said. Since he so frequently visited in the night, and because I primarily worked during the day, I called him Moonlight and he called me Sunshine.

"How's that? How will I find out?" I asked, suspecting the likely answer.

"*Ask!*" he exclaimed.

The next day, I sat down and composed a letter to Brock. Because I felt as if I knew him, the words flowed quite smoothly.

Dear Brock,

Though we haven't met, I feel like I know you. I am sure you've heard about me. I'm the angel lady and I have wings for you.

Your cousin shared with me that you are sick. I am a medium, I can talk with deceased loved ones. Your father has asked me to reach out to you. He loves you and wants you to know he's at your side.

Would you be willing to talk with me? This might seem weird, and if so, I apologize. But I feel compelled to reach out to you.

Thank you. You are very loved.

And that was it. I sent it off immediately, digitally, instantaneously marveling at the wonder of technology. *Waiting. How would he respond?*

The business of the day once again took forefront in my mind; my children had dance class and like Old Mother Hubbard, my cupboards were bare. Off to the store!

That night, with my kiddos nestled down, I tidied up a bit. After the birth of my first daughter, I decided to allow my living room to be a canvas, and each day I would accept the unique masterpiece that would take shape. Somedays the living room teemed with Barbies, overflowed with stuffed animals, burst at the seams with crafty things. Coming to peace, accepting this, took growth on my part.

As a child, I felt lucky because my mom chose not to work outside the home. Yes, we made sacrifices, but her presence was worth more than gold. She took her job as a housewife very seriously, and would often express frustration and exasperation when everything was not just so.

With a toddler, then an infant, then a third in my brood, I quickly learned that every person has a different definition of organization and method of achieving that goal. My oldest likes to collect, and everything is set and displayed just so. My middle child is a free spirit, she kicks off her shoes, sprawls out in the sun, and happily digs laundry out of a basket instead of folding it and placing it in the drawer. My youngest just goes with the flow, he's happy to help when asked, but he would be just as happy with all his set ups, all his pet habitats, each of his pieces of art, on full display and left out.

I decided that my vision of a June Cleaver living room really served no one, least of all me. Why would I value the way our common room looked over how the room could feel? With all the wonder and joy channeled into their work and play, my children decorate with love. I accept this, and cherish it. My kiddos refer to our house as "home."

To get to my workspace in the living room that night, I had to step over a Barbie scene, each doll proudly on display. From what I could glean, the Barbies were camping: sticks from the yard had been crafted into a lean-to and cloth scraps served as sleeping bags. Accidentally, I knocked a Barbie down with my clumsy foot as I stepped over. Carefully, gingerly, I replaced her and apologized. Those little things count.

When, finally, I flopped down on the couch, Mr. Moonlight awaited me.

I looked at him, my heart soft and open. "Tell me about him," I requested. "Tell me about your son. Why would you travel through the ethers to find me, to help him? Please, tell me about your son."

"*He's a gentleman and a leader. He loves the outdoors. He's a cool surfer dude have never, never seen him back down from a challenge. I've seen him cry, too.*

"*He gives so much just because he loves to give and he is full of compassion. He is strong and smart. He believes in himself . . .*" he paused.

After a few moments he continued, "*He believes in himself, but now he's confused. He realizes he's not getting through this. So, he's doubting. That's why I want to encourage him. His journey is not about right or wrong, win or lose. It's about trust, finding peace, and knowing that life continues,*" he finished.

"And miracles?" I asked, seeing reassurance. "That's still the goal, right? Miracle healing, true?"

"*Yes, that is the goal. Thank you,*" his spirit continued.

"Tell me more about him," I invited him once more.

"*I will tell you this: He's different than I am, in some ways. But he had the courage to let himself be who he dreamed he could be. That's why I respect him so much. He's true,*" he concluded.

"Thanks for recruiting me," I said, "I am truly honored. I give you, and him, my heart and all my love. I am here for you!"

For a while, I busied myself with other work; emails from clients, scheduling, administrative duties and the like. I felt a bit sleepy, and decided to take a shower. Before I had a chance to do so, an email from Brock appeared in my inbox.

The text read warm and friendly; he seemed cordial and smart. He expressed his gratitude that I had taken time to reach out.

The last line of the email read, "I'd like to know more; So, even though I don't exactly understand your work, I accept your offer to help me."

I smiled and replied right away, thanking him.

We corresponded a handful of times over the next several weeks. He shared some of his challenges; in contrast, his father's spirit would guide me in spotlighting his triumphs. Concentrated and concise, yet loving and gentle, this approach worked.

Finally, one afternoon, the email arrived. Brock wanted to speak with me by phone. He felt open to hearing from his father's spirit, and to receive the messages he had for him. I felt confident this was the moment of miracles.

CHAPTER 4

The Outskirts

URING MY TENURE as a nurse, I witnessed the cold, dark hand of death and embraced the sweet, soft breath of life. The two forces seemed opposites in medical paradigm: Life defined success, the benchmark of good medicine. On the contrary, death mocked technology, pharmacology, and surgery, sneering at the best procedure and techniques. In no way was death viewed as success.

As a student nurse, I found myself assigned, one cold early morning, to the Labor and Delivery Unit. The pre-shift, wee morning hours had been bumpy for me; this was atypical. My alarm was set for 4:45 am, yet my stubborn ears refused to hear it until 27 minutes into its shrill reverie. Shocked into full wake mode by the red digits glaring ominously at me from the face of the clock, I jumped out of bed and dressed in a mad rush. I streaked a washcloth across my face, ran a toothbrush over my teeth, and put my hair in a *really* messy bun. Remembering the shift typically ran long, I decided to grab something quick to eat on the road.

Yanking a mug from the cupboard, I filled it half way with chocolate soy milk that sneakily sloshed out and dribbled onto my white shoes. *No matter,* I decided, as I dashed to the garage. The car felt cold, and, in my haste, I neglected to nab a coat. I hesitated, considered, then turned the key. "*Oh well,*" I thought, "*I guess I'll be cold today.*"

Thankfully, the drive to the hospital went smoothly; only a few cars peppered the road at that hour. Mid way through the commute, I reached down to the floorboard and fumbled through my purse in search of breakfast. I discovered the foil wrapped toaster pastry sunken at the bottom of my bag like an old buried treasure. Wondering what flavor awaited me, I opened the shiny covering, and took a bite.

Frosted strawberry with pink sprinkles, oh why? The sugar filled my mouth; it was just too much. The overpowering sweetness and the intense flavoring caught my still snoozing taste buds off guard. I half swallowed, then snatched a napkin from the glove compartment. "*I guess I'll eat a big lunch today,*" I thought as I tossed the remaining hunk in the back.

Now, I pulled into the outskirts of the hospital parking lot, I watched the employee shuttle pull out of the bus stop. This meant I would have to walk to work. I huffed, then thought, *it can only get better from here on out.*

Somehow, despite the imperfect start, arrived on time to the floor. I slung my backpack into a locker and one of the nurses called to me, "Student, you better get into Room 5. The mom in there is getting close to delivery. Scrub up! It's go time."

I followed her orders and made haste to the room. Hair in cap, booties on feet, mask correctly donned I looked the part. But I didn't feel it. Something felt strangely wrong.

My body must have indicated this in some way, because one of the techs asked, "Are you okay?"

I spoke, muffled through the mask, "Yeah, just nervous, I guess."

The room suddenly buzzed with rapid but well-orchestrated

activity. The mom was positioned to push as the bed was broken down. I saw a kick bucket slide quickly across the floor as the doctor rolled in on her stool. Nurses were calling out times as the mom began to heave and shout. I felt hot, and my throat began to close.

Everything around me started swirling and I felt as if I were flickering in and out of my body. The periphery filled with dark shadows and I remembered feeling this once before . . . I heard a crash.

"Get up, you need to get out of here," the same tech was looking down at me. I was on the floor.

"Oh, my gosh, what happened, I am so sorry," I sickened with embarrassment. If only I could disappear, or run out the door.

Off in the distance, what felt like millions of miles away, I heard the shrill chords of a newborn filling his lungs for the first time, and the happy strains of a mom seeing her baby at long last. Birth, a life brand new!

I closed my eyes as the tech helped me up and toward the door. Pulling off the mask, I said, "I need some water, or some air. I'm sorry. Something happened in there."

She ordered, "Go to the break room. Come back when you're ready."

I walked down the hallway in a daze, feeling detached and a bit numb. The sensation echoed something I had felt before, yet I couldn't quite put my finger on it . . . that first moment of life.

My knees suddenly buckled as I remembered when I had experienced this before.

It was the moment of my mom's death, the instant her soul sloughed off her body.

I sat down on the concrete floor just outside the break room. What was this? How could that first breath of life feel just like the final sip of air? How? Life and death are opposites. Win and lose, night and day, beginning and end.

Or was it?

"Hi Sunshine!" my thoughts were interrupted by Mr. Moonlight. *"It's called the Outskirts, that place you're thinking about."*

"What do you mean? I wasn't even thinking of a place. And when did you get here? Okay, what's up?" I asked with an eyebrow raised and a playful smile.

"I thought you might like some company, some coaching from a real live dead guy!" he smiled. I could see he was pleased with his own joke.

"I'm all ears. What's the outskirts?" I asked.

"Well, you tell me how you define it," he quipped.

"Okay, the outskirts is the area between the bright lights of the big city and the wide-open spaces of the country. It's where you can easily access the amenities of town and, just as easily, take advantage of the natural landscapes. It's the place between two worlds.

"Often, people could find safety or shelter in the outskirts of town. Sometimes people who are not "typical" or "usual" take residence there. I think of the outskirts as a bit mysterious, wild, or unknown," I concluded.

"Good, so it's a meeting point between two worlds. It's neither the town nor the country. It's the twilight, ombre, the space between, correct?" he asked.

"Yes, I think so. And this is important because . . ." I cued him.

"It's the changing station between this side and the Other Side. It's where you work and where I am teaching you. Musicians meet melodies, writers meet muses, and artists meet living colors in the Outskirts. Dreams are realized, hope is infused, faith is strengthened there.

"The death of your mom and the birth of that baby took place in the Outskirts. You felt the intensity of it, because part of you was swept there, too.

"When you talk to my son, you can give him a glimpse of it. His heart will remember it, because he was there, between lifetimes, many times before. Each of us goes there. When the feeling of eternity is rekindled, when his endless heart remembers, peace will prevail," he concluded.

"Do I use the term? Do you want me to tell him about the Outskirts? I feel a little Wild West Calamity Jane when I talk about it!" I said.

"You don't need to say anything in particular. You just prove to him with messages and words that I am with him. Then he'll get it," Jack's spirit commented.

Suddenly, I felt an exciting surge of energy at a newly experienced revelation, "Does healing happen in the Outskirts? And . . . Miracles?" I exclaimed.

He winked. *"Good job, Sunshine."*

He was gone.

The next day, as scheduled, I placed the call. Hearing Brock's voice was surreal and reassuring at the same time. He sounded pleasant, though a bit nervous. Truthfully, I felt nervous, too.

"It's good to finally talk to you, to meet you," he said. "Thanks for caring and for all your help."

"Oh my gosh, I'm the one who's really thankful. It's nice to hear your voice. How are you?"

He gave me the rundown. He had been out of the country for a few weeks at an alternative healing center. At this place, natural remedies were utilized and emphasis was placed on the mind-body connection. He commented on how relaxed he felt there; the grounds were beautiful.

"What now, then? Do you go in for more treatments? What's next?" I asked.

He explained the meds that had worked and those that had not. He talked about his markers and overall stamina. The nurse in me felt right at home, and I enjoyed implementing the medical vernacular. Then he asked me, "So what do you think of all this?"

I took a deep breath. Though I didn't see Jack, I felt him, right by my side. I said, "I am glad you are open to so many modalities. You are really balancing a lot. I would wonder if you've tried acupuncture?"

"That's so funny you say that, I was just thinking about that. Do you think it would help?" he asked.

"I would suggest finding a good practitioner and giving it a try," I offered.

"Steffany, is my dad around? Is there something to the afterlife?" he asked.

Again, a deep breath. "Your dad is always near you. He is your helper and your guide," I explained.

We spent the next several moments discussing his father. I shared with Brock my impressions of his dad, his charm, personality, and tenacity. Then, I began to share specific details to offer validation.

During this, Brock stayed quiet. I wondered if he understood, if he felt upset, or if he just needed time to take it all in.

Finally, I relayed a message from his father, "Your dad doesn't want you to over-improve the outdoor space on the back of the house. Keep it simple," I explained.

He laughed, "Now I know you're talking to him. That is exactly what he would say!" he laughed.

Jack further went on to chat with his son a bit about how he loved to watch over the grandchildren, how he wanted them to do well in school, and how thoroughly he enjoyed hearing his granddaughter sing. Brock loved hearing about his father watching over his kids. That seemed to give him a tremendous amount of comfort.

In time, Jack's spirit began to paint a picture of the woods that lay just past the football field near the area where Brock grew up. He talked about campfires and trail rides. I could feel the heat and smell the smoke of the blaze. I shared these images, every impression, with Brock. I heard him give a soft sigh.

I closed my eyes. There we were, Brock, his father, and I. Gathered around the fire, on the Outskirts of time. I could have stayed a while.

But the clock in my office beckoned me back to the land of time frames, dead lines, and schedules. I knew it was time to say goodbye.

"Can we talk again?" Brock asked. "I feel really good about this. Thank you for your time!" he said.

"I would like that! Until next time, goodbye!" I stated. And the call was done.

"Whew!" I said to Jack. "That was great! I'm so glad we spoke. He's quite a great guy! You should feel proud.

"That was a step forward," I stated. "I think he gained some ground."

"*Yes, he did. You helped ease his mind,*" Jack said.

"You know, it might be crazy, but this just might work! I am starting to believe," I said. "We can do this! In the Outskirts, miracles, I believe!" I explained.

A week slipped by; I didn't reach out to Brock, even though he was on my mind. Finally, mid-week, I decided to email him, to see how he was feeling. It was time.

He replied through email that he was having a tough go. He had a setback. The disease was raging, and stronger this time.

Reading his email, I felt such sadness; overwhelming compassion for him flowed from my heart. It wasn't supposed to be this way. He could not die.

Suddenly, none of this seemed right.

CHAPTER 5

Provisions

"THE DEAL'S OFF, Moonlight, I want out," I spat the words bitterly as my stomach turned, twisted, knotted. "You can't do this to me. No way. It's hard enough, doing this work."

His silence defied me as my ears filled with the pound, pound, pounding of my heart. I fought tears.

Then he appeared, clad in dark denim and a fitted, white, crew neck T-shirt. On any other night, I would have found this sight enchanting. Tonight, his charm was lost on me.

"*You rang, Sunshine,*" he greeted me with a sing-song voice. "*You seem a bit out of sorts. What's wrong? Tough day at the office?*"

"Listen, I've put myself out there, way out there, for you. Don't mess with me. You know exactly why I'm upset. You know about all the lab reports. What are you doing? Why did you drag me into this mess? This is not a game, you know."

He looked at me with a blank expression. I waited for a moment, then blurted out, "I'm not going to do this if you can't give me some sort of guarantee. I would prefer not to humiliate myself."

Being a medium in the Midwest, living in a conservative, Christian neighborhood, takes a great deal of courage, a tremendous amount of strength, and a whole lot of spunk. Though cultural and religious attitudes have shifted somewhat, most people in my area still seem to regard the psychic arts with a bit of suspicion and uncertainty. I am often met with a raised eyebrow when I talk about my work.

Yet, despite the occasional damnation of my career path by a fundamentalist or two, I persist. I persist because I believe that we are so much more than a body. I share because I know there is always a reason for hope.

Talking with the dead has taught me plenty about life. So often, we allow ourselves to exist in fear, restricted by limits, held back by unrealistic expectations. We hide our light, dim our brilliance, dull our luster because of guilt, shame, doubt. Half asleep, stumbling to rushing, we seem to search and scramble for something to help us out of pain and to relieve us of uncertainty. Too often, sadly, our dreams die long before we leave our bodies. I believe that when we abandon our dreams, when we stop believing, death is only a matter of time.

Oh, but on the Other Side of the physical world, we spring into life! In endless light we grow, heal, learn, forgive, explore, make peace, and let go. All in the blink of an eye. Timeless.

Our loved ones on the Other Side are very much alive! Zestfully, fully, wholly immersed in life, we simply cannot die.

Once, I had a man's spirit explain to me, "*Batteries die. Vacuum cleaners die. Light bulbs die. Me? Not even death could convince me to die! My spirit is alive.*"

I spoke with the spirit of a woman whose adult daughter wanted to reach her. I saw her mother's spirit sitting behind a beautiful grand piano with an angelic master composer at her side. The woman's spirit smiled, and she said, "*Oh, I do so enjoy the afterlife. I finally get to play the piano. With seven children to raise, I never had the time.*" This message proved meaningful for her daughter.

"My mom always wanted to play the piano, but with all of us, she worked every day of her life," she commented. "I am so happy for her. She deserves that. It's her turn. This is her time!"

That day, however, I received a shocking blow. Brock's lab values were off the charts. His weight was up because of all the fluids. The cancer was getting ahead. This was not how I wanted the story to turn out.

Once again, I spoke aloud to Jack, "I agreed to help because I believed you, me, *we* were going to work a miracle for this guy. He has a family who loves him, kids who need him, and friends who respect him. I'm telling you, promise me a miracle, or I don't know if I want to stay involved."

No sooner had I finished my sentence than he began to fade off. But this was not right either!

I stood up from the couch and paced toward the door. The room grew cold. He was gone.

This was the end? I questioned myself. Would I jump ship because we hit some choppy waters? Did he truly promise me a miracle? Was my help conditional, or somehow related to an outcome? When things were clipping along beautifully, when all was movingly swimmingly, I felt happy to help. But now . . . .

"FINE!" I yelled, "Come back. Please, Moonlight, come back. I'm really sorry."

With my next breath, he filled the room with grace, ease, and love. My entire countenance relaxed as I felt the sincerity of his compassion and the authenticity of his love.

"*No apologies. Now, tell me this, what is a miracle? Be honest, because when you tell a lie, the aura around your nose grows!*" he beamed at the silly quip.

I laughed, "Don't tease me about my aura. Okay, miracle. Well, a miracle is something miraculous. Something inexplicable in human terms. Miracles seem to defy explanation. Everybody knows that. Why?"

He spoke again, gently, yet earnestly inviting me to consider, *"So miracles are about the body? A miracle can only be a significant physical event or change?"*

For the next moment, I considered my beliefs about miracles. I remembered as a third grader, at our Baptist church, I memorized the miracles of Jesus. Water to wine, calming the storms, *healing the sick, lame and blind,* raising the dead; he worked magic all by right of the Divine.

Each miraculous act of Jesus was a very physical, measurable, tangible demonstration of a remarkable hand at work. Jesus didn't miraculously get the close parking space at every mall, or miraculously stick with his New Year's resolution for seven whole months. No! He set in motion cellular, physical, radical change for good. He cured and *healed.*

More importantly, though, was a verse that stuck with me from my formative years in Sunday School. Jesus said, John 14:12 "Truly, Truly I say to you, he who believes in me, the works I do, he will do also, and greater works than these we will do."

Jack read my mind, *"Yeah, pretty bold stuff. But you're missing something."*

"I beg your pardon, but I know my Bible. I've got lots of vacation Bible school awards to prove it. I know a miracle when I see one," I playfully shot back.

"So, you are pretty sure a miracle means that he will be physically healed, and since he's not looking like the picture of health, you don't see any miracles."

"Yes, that sums it up. When you asked for my help, I figured this was going to be a miracle healing. I WANT to be a healer, so that means I want to see him HEALED."

"So, you think healing is about the body, too, do you? Physical healing would be a miracle, for sure!"

"Finally, yes! We're in sync. I just know he can heal. And I don't even have to know how, I just know he can. And that's why you've contacted me, right, because he will?"

Time stood still. No words, no thoughts, but I knew. My heart sank.

"Listen to me. I want you to hear me. This is one of the most important things I can ever teach you. Healing is not always about a physical cure. Healing, really, happens when we line up our soul, heart, and mind.

"Sometimes, that means the body rebounds to a normal state of being. Fine. Sometimes, the body has served its purpose, is cast off AND healing has occurred. You've got to let go of healing being strictly about the body. Healing is reclaiming the soul," he explained. *"Reclaiming the soul, opening the heart, and believing! That's healing."*

I considered this. Could it be? Could a person be happy and sick? Can illness coexist with peace and joy?

I remembered a patient I worked with during my tenure as a nurse. I was in a home health care role and had been assigned a home visit to a three-year-old boy with severe physical limitations and delayed speech. The family was extremely poor; as I entered the duplex I was taken aback. The couch was tattered, a leg on the kitchen table broken, the carpet was thread bare.

The little boy sat in the middle of the floor with a few cheerio cereal rings sprinkled in a cup next to him on the right. On the left side sat a stuffed animal, soggy and worn. He smiled hugely as he put a bit of cereal to his plush friend's mouth. He had so little, but with such joy, he shared all.

Another patient's face came to my mind. She suffered a spinal cord injury in an accident at the age of 16 that left her paralyzed from the shoulders down. She told me once, as I was helping her dress, "The accident took my ability to walk, but it didn't take my ability to smile."

Her legs would never be cured, but suddenly, with Jack's insight, I realized that she was healed!

"*Ever hear of Annie Sullivan, The Miracle Worker?*" Jack asked.

"Yes, you know I have. She was amazing," I answered with genuine appreciation for her and her work.

"*Explain to me,*" he invited me.

"Well, Annie Sullivan was a teacher who worked with Helen Keller. Helen was deaf and blind and lost in a dark, silent world. Helen said, 'I felt locked inside myself with no way out,' because of her physical condition. Annie came into her life and changed this . . . she taught Helen to see with her heart and to speak with her hands. She opened Helen's world," I explained. "The Miracle Worker is the movie based on Helen's life and Annie's work."

"*Yes, so Annie taught Helen to see and hear. But did she restore the physical sight or hearing? Did she reactivate Helen's eyes, or rewire Helen's ears? That would be the miracle, right?*" he asked sincerely.

"She didn't have to turn Helen's eyes or ears back on, at least not her physical ones. The miracle was about Love, the way she helped Helen see and hear with her soul, she helped Helen open her heart to life," I smiled. "Wow! And then Helen went on the be a force for change across the globe. She used Annie's love to work miracles of her own. She helped give others sight, with or without eyes!"

"*Yes, her mission, her presence, helped even sighted people take notice to a world easily overlooked: the world of the deaf/blind. She brought vision to and for all. Yet, the miracle was never, never about the body. It was always about the heart and mind,*" he said.

"You are so right. And Helen Keller would not have done

this had her physical eyes been restored. Her miracle was love," I declared.

Jack spoke up, "Now, *what if I told you that Brock is healing because a miracle has occurred?*"

"I would look at the aura or your nose," I joked.

Then, snapped back into the reality of the situation, the truth of what was unfolding, "That sounds a bit far-fetched to me. Remember the lab values? The edema?"

"*Three weeks ago, he thought I was dead and gone. He feared death and didn't really accept the thought of an afterlife. Worse, he was stuck in his body, suffering and feeling alone. He was locked inside himself. Speaking to you, hearing from me, has changed that. He is starting to believe, release the fear and MIRACULOUSLY, despite the raging disease, he feels a deepening sense of peace. Does that seem a bit like healing or sound a little like a miracle?*" he asked.

"Really?" I wondered.

"*Sunshine, he's smiling in the rain. That's a miracle. Or, as you might say, it's a healing.*" he declared.

"But what about the disease and the other stuff? I don't want to say anything bad. I don't want to be giving false hope. I don't want to mess this up! I blew it with my mom, don't let me destroy this," I said.

"*Okay, here's the deal, you don't have to come up with the words. I will speak if you will listen,*"

I replied, "And I will listen if you speak."

"*Deal?*"

"Deal."

He slipped away. The night's lesson was done.

CHAPTER 6

Love

GENTLY, HER LITTLE hand shook my shoulder. "Mommy," she softly spoke, "can I snuggle with you? The sun's almost up," my daughter slid down on to the couch, nestling in close to me.

Sleepily, I fumbled around for a blanket. Though I couldn't be sure, in my hazy state, I suspected that I had perhaps fallen asleep in the wee hours as I worked. My fingers hooked the corner of a blanket, and, as I pulled it up over the two of us, I cracked my heavy eyelids just enough to see the worn clothes on my body and shoes still on my feet. These less than desirable conditions for sleep would have to suffice for a night's rest; the sun beckoned me to the day's tasks.

I laid still a few moments more, appreciating the quiet moment with my girl. She, like me, sees angels. She has since she was only a few months old.

As a baby, she would often stare into the space just over my shoulder and smile with wide eyed wonder. Curiously I would turn my head to observe what she saw, but unfailingly, in a burst of light, the friendly spirit would vanish. Poof! Gone.

One day, she and I were sitting together on the living room

floor. Two years old, she loved to bask in the sunlight. As she soaked, blinking, drenched in sunbeams, she looked past me and said, "Hi!"

I smiled, a bit puzzled, and replied, "Hi!"

"No, no." She began pointing behind me. "She! Hi!"

I felt a chill go down my spine, and I understood she could see a spirit. Without turning around, I said in my mind, "Hello, thanks for stopping by!"

An instant later, my tot waved and cheerily said, "Bye-Bye!"

The openness of children inspires me personally and professionally. So often, parents reach out to me with concerns, questions, or queries about odd or astonishing or amazing behavior on the part of their progeny.

Most children possess a more fluid understanding of life. Seeing the spirit of a departed loved one is much easier for a child; little ones don't have the baggage and trauma wrapped up in death the way most adults do. Additionally, most children have not been conditioned to believe the seeing spirits is evil, weird, or bad. Those are learned lessons, not innate tendencies. We are born connected; we are never really separate from our true home: The Other Side.

But as adults, and super responsible ones at that, we frequently feel the urge to have a solid, good, logical explanation for everything. And if we don't have a plausible reason for a seemingly impossible event, like seeing a dead person, perhaps, sometimes, a well-intended but uneducated parent could introduce fear or the feeling of being "not normal" to a child.

Over the course of my professional career as a medium, I have learned that most children are sincere and truthful when sharing about spirit encounters. Granted, kids can exaggerate, animate, and fabricate when an audience awaits, but a good listening ear, and a heart that doesn't fear the unknown can discern a child's genuine experience from the "story" or an "act."

Our loved ones on the Other Side want to connect with us just as much as we want to connect with them! We don't hold them back, pester them, distract them, or upset them when we seek that confirmation or ask for a sign that their loving presence remains at our side. Just as we teach our little ones who to use spoken language, our loved ones on the Other Side are trained to communicate with us though dreams, numbers, animals, license plates, music, pennies, and a wide array of signs. Love is a language that is universal and learned in the heart.

So, as I cuddled beside her, I wondered if she sensed Jack's spirit, or if she ever saw him around. I dozed off, drifting in and out of a light slumber, then my little boy padded in. Neither my son, nor the sun would be ignored. *"Rise and shine!"* I told myself.

The morning breezed by at an accelerated tempo; I scarcely had a moment to think about lab values, cancer, miracles, or the meaning of death and life. I glanced at the clock: lunch time! Only a precious hour until I had to get to work.

Peering at my calendar, I noted three sessions scheduled for the day. The first was a mother and her two adult daughters; the second, a mother with her thirteen-year-old boy; the third for a lady coming solo. I took a deep breath, easing into the workload. As I exhaled, an early bird spirit showed up. I suspected he belonged with my first group.

Spirits don't wear watches, Fitbits, nor do they utilize any other devices for tracking time. True, some are more punctual than others, because, even after death, our personalities tend to stay true to form, but the anticipation many spirits experience in having the opportunity to speak with their loved ones, using me as their voice, is nothing short of sheer joy. Hence the early bird.

"Helllooo!" he bellowed at me. *"I'm so happy to see you! You look great today!"*

"Flattery will get you nowhere, sir. You must wait for your people. We'll talk then. For now, I should get ready. I'm hungry," I politely explained.

He grinned. I knew I would have my hands full with this one.

"*Well, I've waited six years to talk to them. A few minutes more won't kill me,*" he laughed heartily at his own joke.

Yes, I had my hands full.

His family arrived a few minutes early, and I welcomed them into my office. His two daughters seemed nothing alike: one prim and proper, the other looked like she enjoyed a walk or two on the wild side. Their mother, a woman who appeared to be in her sixties, could have been Aunt Bee from Mayberry. She was very kind and unassuming indeed.

As they sat down and got cozy on the couch, I explained, "I don't know if you've lost your father, but there's a father figure who has been laughing and hanging out for the past hour or so. He likes to smile!"

The trio of ladies looked at one another, burst out laughing, then the mother began to cry happy tears. "That's our dad," confirmed the older daughter.

The session moved along beautifully, with so many amazing validations and confirmations. When I work with spirits, I ask them to be my tour guide on the Other Side. I want them to show me, tell me, let me see what their life is like. Heaven is an etheric fingerprint; unique to each spirit who resides there. I love to see what they see, to smell, taste, feel and know just what they do.

This man showed me grape vines, Mustangs, whiskey barrels and the Florida Keys. He told me about willow trees and tattoos and the music at his funeral. I could see the family members who greeted him on the Other Side, including a child he and his wife lost shortly after birth, a lap dog, a big drooly dog, and a few barn cats. He was loud, vibrant, and unapologetic, living with no regrets. When it was time to leave his body, he slipped away, peacefully, his family gathered in tearful celebration at the bed side. A well lived, much loved life.

As I considered this man, I realized this: His physical death seemed more like a comma before a conjunction, not a period at the end of the line.

He lived a good life, and he kept living, free and happy, on the Other Side.

I closed the session and the ladies left, joyful, comforted, validated, and satisfied.

The youth and his mother arrived next. I loved this young man immediately; his sweet smile and his pure heart radiated goodness and truth. Since I didn't notice and strongly present human spirits around him, I wondered if he had come to see me for some other cause.

He had.

As we sat down, his mother pulled out several notebooks, each stuffed with pencil drawings. She explained, "Since he was little, before he could even know any of this stuff, he has been drawing the engine rooms of ships. Look. The first drawings are crude because he was only four to five. But I never taught him any of this. He was born knowing," she handed me the notebook; I flipped through.

Indeed, detailed drawings leaped from the page. Neatly labeled, clearly marked, I felt as if I was looking at an engineering student's notebook.

"I was there, on the ship, in the engine room, when it went down," he spoke up. "I've remembered this since I was little. I can feel the heat and smell the smoke. Sometimes I feel the panic as the ship went down, too. Do you think it was a past life?"

A vast body of research by psychologists and medical doctors alike seems to support the reality of past lives. In some New Age circles, past lives are quite trendy; all the cool spiritual people have one.

Admittedly, in my early years as a professional medium, I shied away from the whole notion of reincarnation, transmigration, or past lives. This was not out of logic, but rather, from some old lessons taught through fear.

In the mid-1980s, as an elementary student, I attended a fundamental Baptist church with my family. Each Sunday, the pastor spewed fire and brimstone, shouting of Original Sin and entreating us to come to Jesus to save our souls.

One Sunday, standing tall at the pulpit, he waved a book around. "This is out on the shelves now. This woman is in counsel with the Devil. She works with evil forces. She tries to tell us that there are past lives. Do not be deceived. This is Satan's work." I squinted, hoping to view the cover. The face of a pleasant looking woman with beautiful, fiery red hair smiled at me from the platform. The book was Out on a Limb by Shirley McClain. I vowed then and there that I would not, could not, did not believe in past lives. And that was that.

A few months into my mediumship practice, I noticed every time I went to the bookstore, library, or new age shop, a prominent display of materials on past lives would greet me at the door. I choose to ignore this, feeling uneasy with the concept. I declared aloud to the Universe, "I am not at all interested in working with past lives." Done.

Within a few days, I sat face to face with a client who asked, "Can you tell me about my past lives? I am so interested, and I just know I've been around before." The irony of her request did not escape me. I politely skirted around that, putting it back to her, "Where do you think you've been in other lifetimes?"

She launched, quite animated, into some of her dreams and insights about who she'd been, whom she'd been with, and where she had landed. These experiences seemed reasonable to me, and I told her this. She was very satisfied; I had the sense that she didn't need me to tell the story, rather, she needed validation for the wisdom that had revealed itself within her.

The next day, I found myself conducting a phone session with a woman out West. We chatted with her grandfather's spirit, as well as the spirit of her beloved dog. All went well. Then,

"I feel really stuck with money. I think it's a past life issue. Can you confirm this?" she said.

I closed my eyes and grimaced, thankful she could not see my pained expression over the phone. Clearly, I had some inner work to do.

That afternoon, certain as the sun, a third client asked about her past lives. I decided to rework my terms with the Universe, "All right, I'll learn."

The next few months proved exciting, fascinating, revealing, and liberating as I exchanged my fear for simply curiosity. I allowed myself merely to learn; I determined that I need not prove nor disprove the possibility of past lives and reincarnation, rather, I opted to become a studious pupil. This lead me to deeper understandings of the Universe, and our soul. Without trying to make it right nor worrying it could me wrong, I soaked up the materials I uncovered like rich, fertile nutrients for my growing mind and soul.

Some of the literature was like junk food, unhealthy, completely artificial, and bad for the heart. Other, like the work of Dr. Brian Weiss and Dr. Ian Stevenson not only resonated with me, but compelled me to shift my beliefs. My skill set as a practitioner reflected this change of heart; I began "seeing" scenes from past lives in remarkable detail, just like a full color motion picture, when clients would ask.

Wanting to maintain my high standard of professional veracity and integrity, I selected a teacher and gained certification in past life regression and hypnotherapy. Dolores Cannon, a small lady whose work stands in immense stature, conducted the training. I felt truly blessed to have worked with her. She made her transition in 2014.

After working with a number of clients using this type of therapy, I did observe something of concern. Occasionally, a person might become enamored with, or even obsessed by, a past life. This proves detrimental, because it deprives the person of presence, of the moment, where miracles happen and growth occurs. The best gift is the present. This moment is all we need, all we're given, the best we've got.

This youth, a smart, sweet young man, seemed to have an awareness of this lifetime aboard a ship, yet seemed well anchored in his life. He loved to draw buildings and other structures in addition to nautical fare. I asked him, "Have you ever ridden your bike pedaling backwards?"

He laughed, "No, I wouldn't get very far forward."

"Ever walk while looking constantly over your shoulder?" I further explored.

"Ha! No. I'm pretty clumsy. I'd run into a tree," he grinned.

"So, that's what I think about past lives. It's good to know about this life you had on the ship. And yes, I know it's true that you were there. It's real. But let me ask. What will you do about it in this life? How can you use what you know to help you grow?"

He answered immediately, "I will tell you! I remember feeling like the ship was not safe, like there could be improvements in the design. I remember not having the courage to say something because I was not an upper-class person. But I wanted to save the people on the ship.

"That's why I want to design safe buildings and other structures. I want to help in a way I didn't get to that time," he smiled.

"Perfect! You're ahead of most adults I know. Now, are you afraid of the water? Do you have any fears around going on ships or taking a cruise?" I asked him.

"No, not really. I think I had a good death. I wanted to go down with the ship. It was duty and honor. I am not scared," he replied sincerely.

We chatted a bit further. He asked about angels and spirit guides; I provided him a compass of knowledge to assist him navigating the waters of the Spirit world. He and his mother felt encouraged and inspired. And so, did I.

The next session stood in sharp contrast to the previous. A young woman lost a dear, best friend, her soul sister, when she completed suicide. Passionately, hurled into a cyclone of stormy emotions after a breakup, the woman had dropped her two-year-old off at her friend's apartment, went home, and called it the end.

She left no note, no word, no goodbye. Nothing, nothing at all.

I established the connection with the spirit of the young woman who ended her physical body and claimed for herself a new life. She was happy, light, and carefree; the calm after the storm. She spoke of personal details to confirm her living presence with us in the room.

Though her friend was happy, and most certainly relieved in hearing her departed soul sister's words, she needed something more, much, much more.

She needed her friend to come back, to give her a hug, to let her know she was strong enough to move on from the break up. She wanted her friend back in the physical world.

Under guide of the woman's spirit, we together explored what the two friends could learn from one another and how a strong, though different, relationship could blossom and bloom. The spirit explained that planting flowers and roasting marshmallows would be a tradition, a ritual, to help her bereaved friend feel whole.

"That's nice, and I will do that," my client explained, "but nothing can gloss over or make pretty the fact that she had a bad death, an awful ending. She didn't have to die."

I felt a surge of heat pulse through me, reminiscent of the nauseous feeling after a bumpy car ride. A bad death, tragic ending.

What about her life?

I tossed that out to my client, "I wonder if you would be able to remember her living instead of her dying. Don't let the darkness of her death eclipse the brilliance of her spirit's light. She is happy, and the truth is, on earth she had moments of happiness, too."

Something in the sincerity of the request must have struck a chord, she seemed to relax, if only a bit. We closed our time together, and as she left, she thanked me.

"It's a step, I suppose. I think I'll always be broken, but maybe now I'm a little less bruised."

As she left, I shifted quickly into mom mode. Dinner time.

That night, with kiddos tucked in, I sat with a warm cup of tea and reflected. With my first sip, from out of the corner of my eye, I could see the message light blipping, blinking, winking at me from the phone. I had received an email from Brock. He wanted to talk.

"Jack! Mr. Moonlight! I need you," I called into the silence. The day's thoughts of happy lives, good deaths, and tragic endings cast aside, I awaited his reply.

He appeared, and I entreated him, "He wants to talk, what do I say. The lab values, his breathing, he's not well. What do I say, I gotta get it right."

"*Teach him about love. Tell him about life.*"

CHAPTER 7

Bargain

E VEN AFTER 15 years as a professional medium, working daily with the Other Side, Death seems rather enigmatic. Not what happens after a physical transition, but rather, *why* we die. Coming into a physical form takes a huge effort, a lot of planning, and audacious courage. We work to cultivate meaningful relationships, to find community, to forge a path to happiness, wholeness and home. Why, then, does it appear that death capriciously, coldly, harshly steals us away from our work or what we love? Why would a newborn do an about face and return to the ethers? How could a mother leave her young children behind? Tell a parent her teen committed suicide because it was his time? Or God called him? Or it was his soul's plan, some grand design? Predestiny? Punishment? Fate?

Why do our bodies get sick, if we're created by divine design? What is the purpose in suffering if the Universe truly wants us to be happy? What is the point in chronic illnesses, freak accidents, diseases with no apparent cause and no ready cure? Why would Brock, an amazing, smart, and kind husband, father, and son take on a rare cancer? Karma?

I refused to believe this line of thinking. The old paradigms were not enough.

I decided to question Jack; I wanted something more.

"I tell you what," I bargained, "I'll feel much better about all this if you can explain a few things to my satisfaction," I tried to sound firm, which is not my typical communication style. "Please?" I softened.

"I will do my best. I will not hold back. You will know what I know," he assured me. I trusted him, heart and soul.

"Suffering and sickness," I blurted.

He casually smiled, considered, then began.

"Remember those shoes you got not so long ago? The black ones with the high heels?" he asked.

"Uh, yeah, but what does that have to do with anything? This is not a fashion discussion." I replied, off-put by his question.

"Tell me about those shoes," came the response.

"Well, I wanted some real live high heels. Nice ones. I tend to be practical and sensible in my footwear, and I'm not really confident enough to wear hot shoes. But, I had a big talk, a public presentation, and I really wanted to look my best. I shopped online for hours and hours, found what I liked, saved up some money, purchased them, then waited for the box," I explained.

"When I tried them on, at first, they felt so great. And I felt good in them. True, it took some getting used to, but I kind of liked the height and the sleek, fuzzy appearance. Okay, so I felt a bit confident in them. For a little while . . . .

"Everyone, and I mean everyone, complimented them. The trouble is, my feet quickly began to hurt. The shoes were no longer fun. I wanted to get out of them, but I didn't want anyone to think I couldn't hack it in heels. I kept them on until I got home, then I kicked them off. Ugh," I explained.

"Do you think you'll wear them again?" he asked.

"Well, yeah! I went to a lot of trouble, a lot of effort. And they look nice. So yes, I'll suffer because . . . Oh. . . ." I trailed off. I was beginning to sense what he had in mind with this conversation.

"Now, what about those water shoes you have? You know, those fabulous shoes," he laughed. I did too.

"Okay, now you're making fun of me. Yeah, I know those shoes are ugly and weird, and designed to be worn in the pool. But oh, my gosh! It's like a dream wrapped around my foot. I forget I'm wearing them. Everyone, and I mean everyone, thinks they're ugly. But I put them on all the time!" I beamed just thinking of those ugly shoes.

"So, let me see if I get this," I started.

"Don't judge. Don't assume. Never, ever judge another person in death or life. Every person is different. Life is a highly personal, inward driven experience. No one can really know what it's like to be you . . . except YOU," he interrupted.

"So, we all come here, and we select a body. We settle in and people notice us, assess our appearance and so on. But inside, we have our own unique feelings, pains, and triumphs that are not ever truly reflected on the outside. No two people will ever feel alike. It's just not possible, not at all.

"And we all have individual levels of tolerance, endurance, willingness. When it was time for me to take those shoes off, no matter how good they looked on the outside, no matter who I wanted to impress in wearing them, no matter how much money I'd spent, I had to take them off. Period, then end!

"When I took off the shoes to go barefoot, my feet stayed on! I didn't lose that part of me. In fact, I felt better. I had regained my feet.

"Likewise, in life, each person does the best they can for as long as they can. And when it's time, not clock time, but feeling time, we've got to kick off our body and go bare-soul. Soul feels good, because we have the whole of ourselves back again!" I felt excited. This made sense.

"*Never judge. Not death, Not life. Just do what is right and true for you. No judgement. Just love,*" he was firm.

"*You judge death as bad when you define life with age or time. Time is meaningless, really, when you've got eternity on your hands, or feet, to draw from our example. You must stop counting seconds, minutes, hours years. Let go of time,*" he instructed.

My mind wandered a bit. Though simplistic, I thought the shoe analogy might be a good one. Each lifetime, every incarnation, could be likened to a pair of shoes. We choose our physical body to move us through the world of form, and, like different styles of shoes, each life time has a theme, a different mission, a unique course. Across some lifetimes, we may return to similar lessons, to familiar missions, recurring themes because we find comfort, ease within them.

Our body is not the whole of who we are, not in any way; we are endlessly, wondrously more. The body assists navigating the physical world. Some lifetimes are short, others are long lasting. Some lifetimes are arduous, difficult as we wade through the muck and mire and feel tattered, soiled, torn. Others are comfortable, easy, fun. Sometimes we're high end, others we're bare bones.

When we move to spirit, we're not gone. We've just slipped off an accessory that helped us learn about our soul.

The shoe seemed to fit.

Then, Jack brought me out of my thoughts.

"*Death is not bad, the enemy, some force to fear. There's no creepy Grim Reaper. It's not to say that it's good, either. You see, death is merely a change of perspective. It's a doorway between worlds. One world is no better, nor is another worse: different vantage points, different outlook, different views. But same Universe, same spirit, same Love regardless of your location,*" *your experience, your attitude. Death is a shift, nothing more nor less.*

"It sure seems like a big, big shift—here today, gone tomorrow. To use our shoe analogy, shouldn't we have a middle ground? You know, spirit socks," I asked.

"There is a middle ground, or, as you note, you do have spirit socks," he replied.

Like Oedipus solving the riddle of the Sphynx, I considered this puzzle. What is the part of us that bridges the gap between physical body and spirit.

"INTUITION!" I knew the answer. "Our intuition is the mingling point, the melting pot, the merging of heaven and earth. Intuition helps us sense and know Spirit through our physical body. Goosebumps, hunches, visions, dreams, déjà vu . . . woo hoo! We do have a means of knowing the Other Side on this side through intuition.

"Meditation, prayer, yoga, time in nature, and creative expression widen the gap to usher Spirit into the world. In quiet, still moments, we access that connection," I exclaimed.

The movie "Meet Joe Black" flashed in my mind. In early scenes of the film, a wealthy, older gentleman is awakened in the night by chest pains and a throaty but emphatic voice that utters a single syllable, "Yes." This man, never admitting to his family, wondered if he were dying. The answer, which he sensed intuitively, was yes.

So often I work with clients who, even when the death of a loved one is sudden, reflect and realize a trail of subtle clues.

A mother with whom I worked lost her daughter when the girl was sixteen. I spoke with the daughter's spirit, and one of her first messages was, *"She knew. Since I was little, she had a sense of it. She knew."*

Her mother cried, an emotional mix of tears of happiness knowing her daughter's spirit was in attendance and drops of sadness at her loss. Then she spoke, "Since she was a baby, really. She was my third child, and, on the moment I first held her, I knew I wouldn't have her long. I never felt this way with the other two children. No matter what, I couldn't shake the feeling. Something in me just knew."

On another occasion, I met with a young woman who sought connection with the spirit of her brother. After his spirit spoke, confirming many happy memories and telling silly jokes, he made mention of this: "*I told her. For a good many years, I told her I would not be around for a long life. I told her.*"

She confirmed, "He did tell me; I didn't want to listen. About three years before his death, he would make comments: he said he wouldn't be around forever, he knew he would never grow old. Weird, gloomy things like that. I wanted to shrug it off. He knew. He knew."

Our intuition couples us with spirit, lets us dance with our soul. When we learn to listen, to pay attention, intuition guides us home.

"*There is no shame in death. It's not a defeat nor a victory. Death is a pause to regroup, assess, make inventory, take stock. A hop, skip, and jump between worlds,*" he explained.

"And what about illness? Surely that's bad?" I asked him.

"*Listen to me,*" he spoke with genuine conviction, "*You spend too much time trying to define. You want to put meaning, rhyme, and reason to every sneeze and sniffle, every bump and bruise, every tremble and tremor. But the truth is this: Illness, disease, and death mean exactly and only what you decide. YOU assign value, purpose, and explanation to these things. The Universe does not have a handy dandy pocket guide to illness and death. That's the blessing or the curse in it; your disease, you define.*"

I considered this and the face of a client came to mind: a middle-aged woman who had been diagnosed with breast cancer, her medical outcome guarded. She explained it to me this way, "I got a call. It came in through my breast. The call told me I needed to take better care of myself. I heard it and accepted. It was my wake-up call."

I remembered the spirit of a man whose daughter came to visit me. He had been diagnosed with colon cancer, but decided it would have no bearing on his life. He told no one and changed nothing about his routine. Only when his symptoms were obvious, when the cancer was far progressed, did he admit to the diagnosis. Three days later, he shifted his energy to the Other Side.

Too, I thought of my mom. There was no plausible explanation for her illness, no just cause. But after the shock of the diagnosis abated, she quoted her favorite movie, The Shawshank Redemption, "I guess it comes down to a simple choice really. I can get busy living or get busy dying."

"*Yes, it's always simply a matter of choice. No matter the circumstance, despite the situation, life is always a matter of choice,*" he said.

I asked, "But why do we have to die? I mean, why does it hurt so much to say goodbye? Why do babies, kids, young people die?"

"*Why do you judge death? Can you set the judgement aside? Are you willing to judge, to suffer, when someone shifts their energy, changes perspective to align with the Other Side?*" he asked.

This question stung me. "It hurts to get left behind," I cried. "When my mom made her transition, I knew she was happy, free, light inside. But I felt DEAD. I didn't know what to do. A big piece of me had died."

Saying these words, I realized part of the difficulty in saying goodbye was because I had no resources, no instructions, no concept of how to adjust my perception, to shift my perspective to align with her vantage point on the Other Side. If she stayed in a physical form, I would not have had to adjust, to let go, to relearn. Life could continue at my level of comfort and familiarity. Safe, stable, known.

When our loved ones shift from physical to spirit, when the change in perception occurs, the sheer Life Force that greets them, that entreats them, that gloriously sweeps them up in a wondrous, sumptuous feast of light is irresistible. Image the most magical sunset, then enrich the colors one hundred-fold. Think of the music that stirs your heart, then picture the notes and chords swirling all around you, singing to every fiber of your soul. Picture paradise, then punch it up beyond anything you've ever seen in this world. Call to mind everything that inspires, delights you, brings you peace. Deepen it endlessly, then deepen it more. Life!

The adjustment to life on the Other Side is effortless, innate, and instantaneous. Partaking of the light, receiving of the unconditional love is easy, a treat for our souls.

There's no learning curve, no adjustment time. Our loved ones awaken completely, mind and soul, on the Other Side.

And on this side? In the aftershock of that change, we resist. We protest. We longingly yearn for the sameness. Just one more touch. Just one more smile. Just be who you were.

If we could learn to shift our perspective, we could never feel dead inside. By accepting and understanding that spirit is always a part of us, not apart from us, we can learn a new language spoken from the heart. We must anticipate and welcome our loved one's presence instead of reinforcing the physical absence. Then, the Other Side opens to us, here, on this side.

We never die; we simply redefine our presence.

Our loved ones reach out, but not from a cloud in the sky. Our loved ones reach out from within our hearts! The memories, the light, the love is always within, without end.

My most heartfelt desire, as a medium and a fellow traveler

on the path, is to help awaken those seemingly dead parts of our heart when a loss has occurred. We are here for life. Despite the pandering of panic and fear, there is no end to our spirit, no limit to our soul.

"I want to make sure I've got this," I was mumbling to myself. The concepts were deep and the notions were wide. I needed a tool, a token, to symbolize and synthesize this concept about life and death and learning to commune with loved ones on the Other Side.

I thought . . . tumbling ideas. Nature, spring . . . grass, trees

"WISH FLOWERS!" I said aloud, proudly.

"The dandelion enters the last phase of its life cycle and generates fuzzy, wispy seeds. When the time is right, when the plant dies, the wind carries the seeds and rests them on the ground. Over seasons, with sun, rain, rich earth, darkness, and trust, the little seeds will root, shoot, and grow into the light. The seeds grow!"

"*So. . . .*" He encouraged me on.

"So, when our loved ones leave the physical world, when the body dies, seeds of spirit are nestled in our hearts. It takes time, not years and months, but seasons and cycles for the seeds to sprout. The cycles and seasons are the first birthdays, holidays, the first anniversary, the big moments and milestones without our loved ones physically by our sides. The sun, rain, and earth represent acts of self-care. We must give ourselves, and therefore those little seeds inside, lots of love, inspiration, rest, good food, and all manners of self-care. We grow the connection to the Other Side through love and nurturing the inside of our hearts!" I declared.

After a pause, a rich, timeless moment for reflection, a wave of readiness washed over me.

It was time.

I grabbed my phone and sent Brock a text.

"Ready to talk," I typed.

Within a few minutes, "Yes."

I dialed his number. He answered, with a soft voice that sounded strained but tired.

"How are you?" I asked him.

"I'm puffy, but I'm alright," he replied. "The kids are busy, and my mother in law arrives tomorrow night. I'm glad for that; I won't have to do laundry!"

I listened to him, keeping a smile on my face. His father's spirit stood at my side.

After a few moments, his father spoke up,

"*Please, tell him I love him. And remind him, I'll meet him on the Other Side.*"

CHAPTER 8

Angels

"Can I ask you about something, Steffany?" Brock spoke quietly; I sensed hesitancy in his voice. Warmly I invited him.

"Please, ask whatever you want to. I am here to help however I can," I replied with a great deal of sincerity. Though part of me feared he might ask about if he would die, or if a treatment would be available, or if he would make it through this, my heart felt a deep sense of peace knowing that whatever he asked, I would be supported with an answer.

From the corner of my eye, I saw Jack's spirit wink. Always on point.

"I am happy to know about my dad. I really am a believer. It's funny how the signs have been there all the while, I just didn't take the time to notice them. Life is so busy, and I had so much going on. I guess it was easier to just keep pushing forward, never considering that he was with me, helping to encourage me and keeping me strong.

"Don't get me wrong, I appreciate that. I'm just wondering about something else. Do you believe in angels? Are there some beings who help us? My dad couldn't be looking after me as a spirit guide before he died. Was I alone? Do you believe in angels?" he asked.

Ah, angels! My heart swelled with love and happiness as I received his questions. Angels inspire us to make an ordinary existence and extraordinary life of Love. Angels are simply love.

My understanding of these spirit helpers has developed and grown over time. As a child, angels were tree toppers, cloud hoppers, puffy, fluffy sky rompers who played harp and sing in some sort of heavenly choir. Though I saw angels drawn or depicted individually, "the angels" seemed to exist categorically as a heavenly mob sent to help humans stranded on the side of the road.

In my fourth-grade Sunday school class, I asked the teacher if she believed in angels. She said, after an awkward pause, "Why, yes. But it's demons we have to be on the lookout for."

"Oh, well, does my kitty have a guardian angel?" I asked.

"Well, no. Why would God waste an angel on a pet? That seems ridiculous to me!" she laughed at the idea.

My cat, a petite gray tabby, the first animal I had felt close to, had been sick. I wanted to pray for her, but didn't know the protocol for asking God to heal animals. I had the idea that perhaps angels could assist on this matter, since God was surely too busy. Clearly, hearing my teacher, my notion was all wrong.

Several months later, the preacher delivered a fiery talk on the fallen angels and Lucifer. The story, set in Heaven before God created the Earth, told of an angel who wanted the throne. In a Roman-esque fashion, he garnered support from power hungry angels and plotted a coup. God got wise to the plan and tossed Lucifer out on his ear, deep, deep down, into the molten core of the earth, into the Lake of Fire. Those angels who supported Lucifer, whose hellish name was now Satan, were cast out as well.

This I knew. And it scared me. But still, I knew nothing much of angels.

In high school, I happened upon a copy of "Reader's Digest" at my grandparent's house. I flipped through the pages when in image caught my eye. A bright burst of light with a dove in the centered in the brilliance headlined the page about "Heavenly Encounters." I devoured the stories, true testaments, from people around the country who had experienced extraordinary assistance or guidance in remarkable ways. I was fascinated, captivated. My curiosity piqued, for sure.

I checked out a few books about angels from the library, and still, these beings remained rather mysterious, too ethereal to clearly define. Angels slowly slipped from interest; too vague, too diffuse to define.

In my mid 20's, years after my mom died, I decided to enroll in a class on spirituality and intuitive development. The class appealed to me because it was nicely organized and seemed very streamlined. The class agenda looked like this

Week One: Spirit Guides
Week Two: Numerology
Week Three: Angels
Week Four: Tarot and Divination Tools

Admittedly, the second and fourth weeks smacked of the Occult, and I looked over my shoulder as I entered the building on those nights. I prayed I wasn't being led down dark path, or the wrong path. I hoped I wouldn't hit a dead end.

Toward the end of the first class, we partnered up to see if we could connect with a spirit guide. I paired off with a lady about my age. I was in for a surprise!

I communicated frequently with my mom's spirit. She revealed herself in dreams, would send messages through songs on the radio, would send signs. One day I walked into a sandwich shop, thinking of her, and looked up. There before me stood a display of "Miss Vickie's Potato Chips." That was her name, the correct spelling, too. Clearly, she traveled by my side.

I never considered the ability to connect with a spirit could go beyond she and I. Why would I?

So, the instructor encouraged us to take a few deep breaths, be quiet, then listen to whatever messages might be expressed for our partner from a spirit guide. I volunteered to "listen," first. My partner sat quiet and wide eyed.

Suddenly I felt a surge of electricity and words started pouring out of me. I could see images, hear sounds, it was incredible, amazing, almost unbelievable. Nearly everything I told her made sense. I had an inroad to the Other Side. I could see the light!

I studied and learned and meditated and prayed and discovered, once again, angels. This time, I realized angels offered a unique, powerful, heart-centered presence as spiritual guides.

I further explained to Brock, "Angels are standard issue in our lives. We all have personal, unconditionally loving, present angels who accompany us through life."

He asked, "But are they human spirits? Pets? Or something else altogether?"

"YES!" I replied enthusiastically.

"Yes, to which?" he laughed, but sounded a bit confused.

"Yes, to all. I used to think that angels were never human, that angels could only be spirit. Sure, an angel can take human form in an emergency or crisis, but an angel would never live an entire human lifetime. This is true," I spoke.

"But our loved ones who have passed can also be distinguished as angels. I've seen that, too," I continued.

The first time I witness this was in a session for a young

woman. She wanted to connect with her Granny's spirit. Her grandmother had helped raised this woman after her parents' divorce at age five.

I connected with her grandmother's spirit. The woman was buxom and boisterous, filled with zeal. She loved her granddaughter very much. After validating her presence with names, birthdays, and other significant information, her grandmother stood sideways and instructed me, "Tell her about these babies! I can fly!" she showed my wings fixed along her back.

Now, I was a young medium, and, being a studious, diligent practitioner, I had very tight parameters and very clear boxes into which I put spiritual guides. Human spirits were guardians, angels were angles, guides were guides. Rules are rules, the comforting, clear standard to which I chose to abide.

I remarked back to the old woman's spirit, "You're a human spirit. You can't be an angel. You SHOULD be a spirit guide,"

She laughed, "*If you try to define, spirit will defy! We don't worry about labels on the Other Side.*"

"Well, then," I said back, "You don't need wings to fly! If you're spirit, why the airy fairy wings to float and fly?"

"*True, and we don't eat, drink, or smoke either. But we show these thing to you. These are symbols, expressions, means of communicating consistency, demonstrating personality. Life is different, but our essence is the same on the Other Side,*" she beautifully explained this to me.

I delivered the message to her granddaughter, "Your granny wants me to tell you she has wings. She shows them to me now. She is your angel and will always stay by your side."

The granddaughter smiled, tears welling in her eyes, "My granny loved angels, and before she died, she promised she'd be mine, Thank you, Granny! I love you!"

Angels represent the part of us that is innocent, pure, filled with light, free. When we make space for angels in our spiritual practice, we choose to feel joy, to accept peace, to find genuine comfort of unconditional love. Angels will never force opinions on us, not heavy handedly guide us. Angels do not judge, compete, nor compare. Angels love. Only love.

The value in acknowledging the presence of angels comes from the feeling we derive from their goodness, purity, devotion, hope.

Angels can appear in white robes, ripped jeans, rock and roll t-shirts, or Bermuda shorts. Whatever we need to see, in the way that is most comfortable for us to perceive, angels will always dress the part. When it comes to love, angels wear it well.

Brock asked, "Do angels have names? Do I need to call them? Steffany, what's my angel's name?"

I quieted my mind. The light that shone around Brock pulsated in waves of sparkling white. Around his chest and head, dense around his body, his energy field looked heavy, sludgy brown black. I sensed very clearly that the cancer was dark and ugly, relentless and unflinching. Covering that, like a lace veil, was the golden lattice of an angel's essence. I heard a voice, feminine and strong, "ANGEL."

I reported this, "Well, you can call your angel Angel."

He chuckled, "That's easy to remember. Listen, I want to thank you. I know it's late for you."

I looked at the clock. It was midnight. The time zipped by.

"My wife would like to talk to you. Do you have time?" he asked.

"I will look," I pulled up my schedule, "I can squeeze her in tomorrow for a bit of time. Will that work?" I offered.

"I'm sure it will be fine. Thanks again. I feel really different. I feel peaceful. I think I'll sleep well tonight," he commented.

"Thanks, me too, "I replied. "Goodnight."

I hung up the phone. I sat quiet for a long time. Something was different.

I understood. And as I drifted off, a single thought danced in my mind:

Miracles.

My first session the next day was for a lady and her sisters. We spoke by phone. The woman, middle aged, was at home on hospice care. When her sisters booked the appointment, they were uncertain whether she would be physically present to attend the session. Weak and soft spoken, she rallied enough strength to talk with me. She wanted to speak to the spirit of her deceased father to make sure he was waiting to meet her.

He was a strong, chatty spirit, the sort who makes my job as a medium easy. I liked his honesty and his down-to-earth demeanor; a practical spirit if ever I met one. He offered many validations, then provided some wonderful, loving guidance.

"Please let my daughter know that she has time to do something wonderful for her children. Ask her to get a stuffed animal for each. She can fill each toy with all her love, her wisdom, her strength, her essence. Then, after her transition, the children will have something to hold and to hold on to. This will be a gift to help them accept she will always be there with them, even from the Other Side," he explained.

His spirit concluded, *"And please tell her I'll catch her, I'll greet her when it's time. Her baby and the dog, too. We'll welcome her with open arms on the Other Side,"* he smiled.

These messages touched me deeply. When her children longed for a physical connection, the plush animal would allow them to hug and squeeze and cling to a symbol of their mom's undying love.

I had a fleeting thought of sharing this with Brock's wife, sensing she could apply the message to benefit her and Brock's children. I wrapped up with the sisters, then gave his wife a quick buzz.

She asked me about Brock's state of being and wondered if she should have hope. She needed to know if I could see a new treatment that might help, or if I sensed on old treatment they might have overlooked. Nothing came to mind.

"Should we go out of the country? I don't think he would make it. But I would do anything to make it work," I could hear her sniffle.

"What would you want? What would you like to do?" I asked her.

"I want him to be alright. That's all I want. I want the love of my life to be alright! Please, tell me you can help us. I need to have hope," she said.

"I know you're all working so hard. Brock looks very bright," I told her. "He is a strong man. Trust him. And take care of you," I reminded her.

We spoke to a few of her loved one on the Other Side, then I had to go.

"You're not alone in this, I assure you. You have angels on your side," I spoke.

We agreed to speak again over the weekend. I forgot to mention about the stuffed animals.

When she and I spoke again, we had an entirely unexpected conversation. Brock had taken a turn for the worse. In haste, he was rushed to the hospital. Ever-nearing the end of his physical life, Brock prepared to go Home.

CHAPTER 9

Together

I COULDN'T SLEEP.

The room was too hot and too cold. I felt tired but wired, hungry and full. Something was under my skin but hanging heavy over my head. I couldn't put my finger on it, but something was amiss or afoot. I was quite distraught.

My mind wandered through time, traveling the past, until memories of that day in the ICU overtook me. I could see myself slumped in the chair of a windowless waiting room, waiting for my mom to die.

A nurse from the unit had come in to update my family; Mom was breathing about three times a minute, shallow sips of air. She would go at any time, and we were advised to say goodbye.

I slipped into a private bathroom and locked the door. Sitting on the floor, I looked to the ceiling, up into the fluorescent light. I started to pray, "Dear God . . ."

At that moment, something overtook me and the prayer passed away, taking another form. From deep within me, like a smoldering volcano, erupted angry words from the darkness of fear.

"How could you do this, GOD? You greedy monster! How could you take her, when you have everything? You don't need her. I do. She's my MOM," I bitterly spat the words through tears.

"She has done nothing to deserve this. HEAL HER NOW. Do not take her, God. Do not!" I demanded unapologetically.

I remembered feeling utterly helpless and totally out of control. Like a tiny row boat against massive tidal wave, I could see my mom swallowed up. Yet tenaciously, stubbornly, defiantly, I held on to some crazy, wild hope. Like the little boat, maybe, perhaps she could make it out alive.

The rage against God began to subside as I crashed onto the floor. A few moments later, after I had collected myself, I knew she was gone.

A tear rolled down my cheek as I sat remembering this; and the feelings washed over me anew. Was Brock dying? Had I failed again? I called out, softly, "Jack . . . . . . Mr. Moonlight?"

He didn't answer. He wasn't around.

I prayed quietly, "God, please, let it be a physical miracle this time . . . .."

Hope.

After being stabilized in the ER, Brock had been transferred to ICU. While his wife family and awaited the room assignment, they decided to walk the hallways for a moment or two.

His wife and mom wandered together when a chaplain stepped seemingly out of nowhere and into the hall.

"Can I help you," he asked kindly.

"We're looking for a patient," came his wife's reply.

"He's in that room," the man pointed to a room down the hall. "They're taking good care of him. We are praying for him. Take comfort. Know he is in good hands tonight," he said.

The ladies thanked him and moved toward the designated

room. Looking back, Brock's wife noticed the mysterious chaplain had disappeared. Gone.

After a brief pep talk, I convinced myself to get in the shower. I thought the warm water might soothe my spirits and help me calm down. I gathered my supplies and stepped into the bathroom, turned on the portable heater, closed the shower stall door, and let the water cascade down my face and shoulders. After a few moments, I reached up to grab the soap. A blinding light shined all around me. Catching my breath, drawn aback, I heard an enormous "Pop" and reeled at a tremendous expansion in my heart. *What happened?* I wondered.

Strangely, the *pop* reminded me of the night my water broke when I was pregnant with my son. The rush of heat, the surge of energy, that chill up my spine had returned. Just as before, in the moment before his birth, I felt a burst of life.

A few prolonged minutes more and I shut off the faucet, opened the door, and stepped onto the bath mat.

Then, I saw him.

I beheld THEM.

Together, father and son.

Ecstatic joy, wild bliss, the mood was high as the son shone bright. Quickly the scene faded, but in my heart, I knew. Brock was home.

A few moments later, I saw my mom's spirit, radiant, beautiful, standing tall. She looked so light and happy. I hadn't seen her that way in a long while.

Miracles.

I realized that night that death is not a failure. I forgave myself for my mom's loss; I had carried that burden far too long. I hadn't screwed up, disappointed her, nor let her down. How could I have? She's still around, thriving, happy, home.

We're not marred by the mistakes we make; life is marked by the journeys we take from the heart. We live, learn, and grow.

I spoke with Brock's family the next day, and a week later, I had the honor of speaking with his kids. His spirit was easy to talk to, his essence bright. Through me, he shared meaningful messages for all his family. I pray they will nurture those message seeds and grow them for years to come.

That year, I planted flowers for Brock, next to the purple and pink impatiens I put down for my mom. I will continue always to do so.

Because, just like the flowers, the trees, you, me, life is a miracle of Love. And Love lives.

Love lives.

GROWING WISH FLOWERS
Afterword

A T THE AGE of six, he was the youngest person whom I'd had the privilege to serve. His grandmother, a beautiful, benevolent, and busy woman, transitioned a few months prior to our session. His mother and older brother joined.

That afternoon, a perfect Midwest spring day when all the trees are budding chartreuse; the grass blades wave lazily, lime green and lush; the bright feathers of the cardinal pale in comparison to it's bright, bursting tune, the family sat with me, hearts open wide. The elderly woman's spirit spoke,

"When I was there, with my body, I could only be in one place at a time. Now, I can be with each of you all, all the time. I am with you, growing and guiding, and always will be."

Many years later, I saw that young boy, grown into an incredible young man. He smiled at me warmly. I didn't recognize him; he'd changed a bit. He hugged me saying, "I will never forget my time with you. Your messages planted seeds in me, I have grown!"

Today, he facilitates a Nature School for children, where he teaches young people to listen to the spirit of the land, to bless the waters, and to observe the wisdom of animals, and to appreciate the unending wonders of our always loving, ever yielding Mother Earth.

When we leave our body, our values, our words, our vision, notes of our essence are sown in the hearts of those we love. Just like the wafting wisps of the wish flower, the seeds of spirit will grow, and thrive, in the right conditions.

Connecting with our loved ones takes patience, nurturance, light, and love.

Patience is the deliberate choice to willingly allow our loved one's spirits to communicate in right time. When we make the transition from physical to non, we learn a new language and operate under a new set of rules. Additionally, our loved one need a bit of time to rest, review, and renew on the Other Side.

When we shift our focus through the physical death, we change our approach to life too. Those first moments on the non-physical realm are spent reuniting with those who have gone before us, then just being, being in the moment, being still.

After that time of reunion and rest, we have a chance to review the life completed. Flashes, memories, understanding, compassion characterize the life review. This gift, to look at our choices, our path, our experiences, through the eyes of *love* allows grace, freedom, and forgiveness to flow. Therefore, the spirits I communicate with don't hold onto a grudge, or keep track of all the wrongs. The Other Side, in providing us the chance to review, liberates us from the limitations, restrictions, judgements. Healed to whole.

Then, we have a time to restore to our perfection, our fullness, the complete and balanced expression that we are in truth. On the Other Side, we see the pieces put together, we remember the forgotten dreams, we reclaim all the broken parts, learn, understand, release, just let go. This takes time.

After the rest, review, and renewal, we have the chance to

create. We divinely design our own experience of paradise, we create classrooms, we sing, dance, build, discover; each moment is something new. Here we learn to traverse the Outskirts, to visit dreams, to manipulate physical objects, to use the natural world to connect with those left behind. This time for our spirit is expanding and exciting and invigorating. We truly come to life!

Yet, this the time for patience for those on this side. We affirm and reaffirm that we are connected to our loved ones on the Other Side, not merely hope or wonder or wish. We must KNOW we are always connected, inevitably and eternally. Knowingness fosters patience. Give yourself some time.

Here are some inspired steps you can take to patiently allow your loved ones to have time:

Listen to your favorite music
Make a soundtrack of your loved one's favorite songs
Try a new class—something that is purely for fun
Declutter one closet
Redecorate a bathroom
Spend time with homeless pets
Volunteer
Keep a doodle book
Make lists of then make your favorite foods
Get a coloring book
Visit a local museum
Hang windchimes
Fill bird baths
Walk and exercise
Find a pet rock
Take a Sunday drive
Play ball
Take pictures of the sunset

Plan trips, even if you don't intend to take them
Find a child from a different country to be a pen pal.
Light candles
Open the windows and let in the sunshine
Breathe
Relax
Meditate
Read
Pray

Any of these activities will place you in the flow of life. Patience will effortlessly come to you when you're effortlessly, joyfully living life.

The next essential step in growing wish flowers, in connecting with our loved ones, is nurturance. In short, this means you willing take good care of your mind, body, and heart. Sleep when you're tired, eat when you're hungry, cry when you're sad. Be kind to yourself; you need the energy to grow those seeds. Give to yourself and the seeds will sprout. Take time for you.

Sometimes, in the darkness of grief, loss, or separation, our motivation to care for ourselves bottoms out. If you feel you are falling, or your appetite for life is failing, reach out. Sometimes a friend, a pet, a journal, a therapist can be like a fertilizer for barren soul soil.

I truly believe that time spent in nature is one of the most single valuable but grossly overlooked means of self-care. Nature has an incredible way of helping us find balance within ourselves. Trees lend strength and rootedness. The waters renew. Flowers heighten our senses. The sun generates life. Nature will unquestioningly nurture you.

Meditation, too, is a frequently overlooked means of self-care. Meditation allows us to unplug from the drama, and to find a sense of quiet within. If you're new to meditation, an easy way to start is to find a single focus, say the sound of a fish tank bubbler, the whir of an air conditioner, the chugging of a washing machine. Pay attention to this outer sound for as long as you can, and nothing else. After a few moments, you'll notice that you're more relaxed, and your thoughts can slow down. Mediation can truly be that simple. Focus, pause, slow thoughts. The benefits of this are incredible.

Along with patience and nurturance, light is vital to grow seeds. We need sunshine to survive, but light is so much more. Light, in the wish flower garden, means taking an easy, gentle approach to spirit communication.

When we don't see our loved ones, or don't feel their spirit, too often we sink into heaviness. Defeating thoughts, depressed mood, an indifferent approach to life hinder us, hold us down. The light approach allows us the see that life is ongoing, we are growing, and each day we can choose to start anew.

Affirmations bring light. Like little beams of the sun, affirmations shine happily on our hearts and let wish flower seeds grow. Affirmations are empowering statements that remind us of truth.

Here are some gentle, sunbeam affirmations to give you a start

"I am"
"I see life all around me now."
"I am recognizing my growth."
"I accept that my loved ones are with me."
"I love to learn in my own time."
"I let myself breathe."
"I enjoy receiving good."
"I am ready!"
"I allow good in my world."

These types of statements truly help. Use these daily, and write some of your own. You may not feel or see a difference at first, but soon, you will feel a quickening as the spirit in you grows.

Finally, with patience, nurturance, and light, comes love. When it comes to nature, there is a mystery, a magic to the timing in which a seed will grow. Take a packet of seeds, put each seed in the ground, and, despite all things being equal, each will sprout in a slightly different time frame, in its own time. That's the wonder of nature, and with wish flower seeds, it's the power of love.

Each day, focus on *a part*; that is, remember that your loved ones are always *a part* of you, not apart from you. This helps shift the focus from separation to unification, from sadness to oneness, from feeling lost to finding home.

Remember to focus on life instead of obsessing over death. Death is a change, yes, an end, NO! Regardless of what stops a body, nothing can halt spirit, and death will never block the incomparable light of the soul. Our loved ones are living and living well. So, too, must we. We must choose to grow.

So patiently nurture yourself with light and love. The seeds have been planted. Let the presence of spirit, in you grow.

I send love to you. Thank you for choosing life. Thank you for being love.

With blessings always, Steff

Made in the USA
San Bernardino, CA
24 February 2020